Self Portraits

THROUGH THE AGES OF ART HISTORY

LYNN RICHARDSON

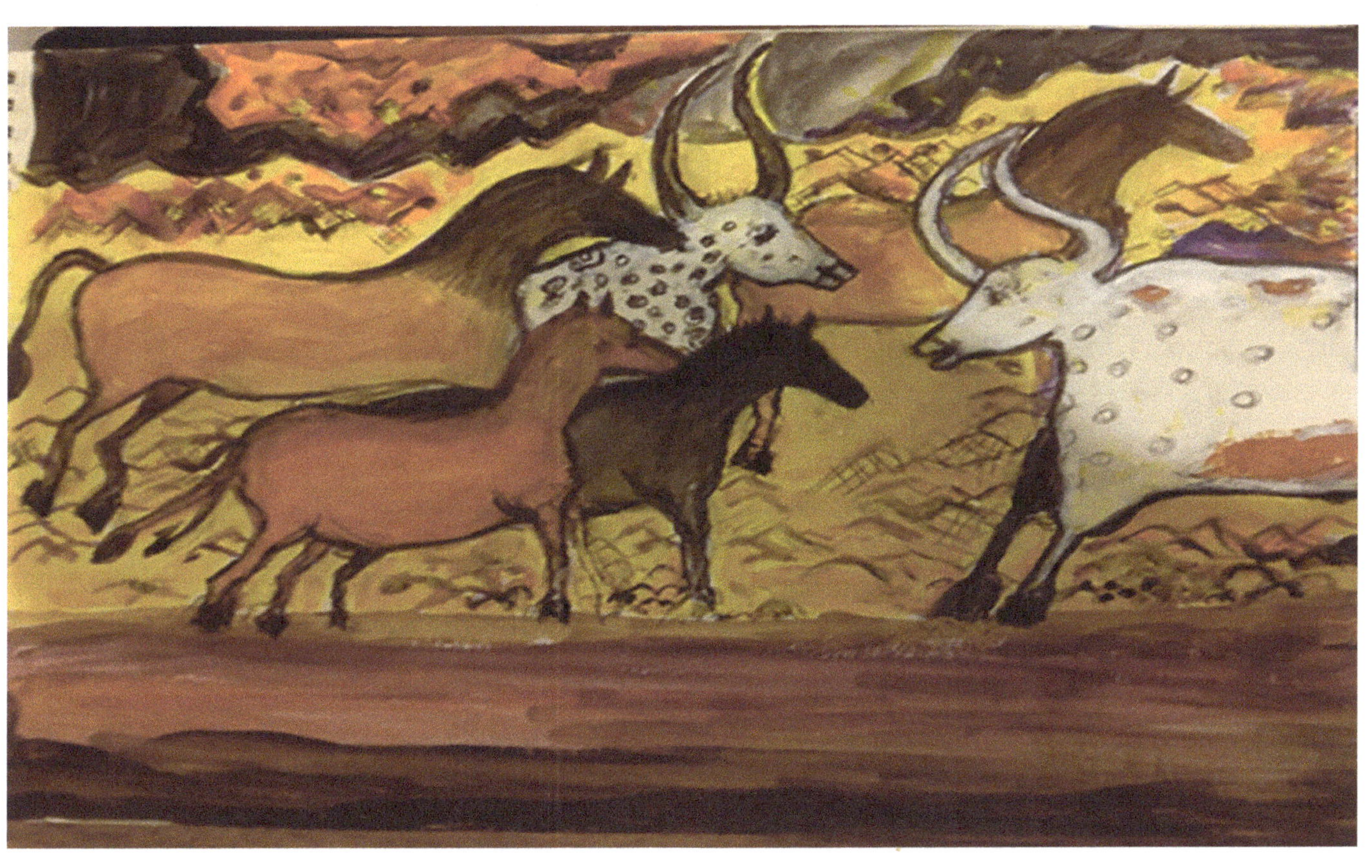

LESSON PLAN FOR DAY ONE
1.5 HOURS - 90 MINUTES

NAME OF LESSON: Exploring Art From The Caves of Lescaux

GRADE LEVEL: Junior College

SUBJECT: ESL/Art

COURSE OVERVIEW: Self-Portraits Through Ages of Art History is a course that will provide context for English language Learners to experience self-discovery through the venue of art. When art is incorporated into the ESL core curriculum it enhances students' engagement and comprehension, increases whole-brain activity, and challenges overall growth in the learning process.

COURSE OBJECTIVES: Upon completion of this course the student will be able to identify and recognize six periods of art history, learn new vocabulary, and be able to express their feelings through the written word, oral discussions, and experience self-discovery through the venue of art. They can make interdisciplinary connections as they explore the life and times of self-portrait artists and create their own self-portrait from the perspective of different time periods and artists. Students can create an artistic work that is entirely unique and gain a sense of accomplishment.

EDUCATIONAL STANDARDS ADDRESSED:

Overview and Intro to Syllabus	10 Minutes	Instructional Input	Explanation of course, syllabus, requirements, and explanation of self-portraits. Student's self-portraits will be used to demonstrate how their feelings and experiences can be reflected through their artwork. Students must discuss feelings and choose images which express their personalities of the artists they choose starting from the Prehistoric period of artwork from the Caves of Lescaux
Short Wood-Cock Munoz or similar test to assess students' level of English proficiency The Woodcock-Munoz Language Survey Revised (WMLS-R) includes a quick and easy-to-ad- minister screener (four tests), and a more- comprehensive 7-test battery, both designed to measure language proficiency of English language learners (e.g., ESL students). The seven tests that comprise the WMLS-R measure the critical area> of listening, speaking, reading, and writing	15 Minutes		Following instructional input, students will be given short assessment test in order to determine whether they are at the beginning, intermediate, or advanced level of English proficiency.

Ice Breaker Activities	20 Minutes	Guided Practice	Students can have a question and answering session and learn from one another's culture, likes, dislikes and customs… What do they enjoy doing the most, what kinds of art do they admire, etc.? Guide students in discussions and have them study images from the pictures of the mural art from the Caves of Lescaux. What images would they like to depict that would *best* describe their personalities?
YouTube Video/Materials on Caves of Lescaux	20 Minutes	Vocabulary: Artist, self-portrait, representation, image, self-expressive art, mural, pre-historic	Students break up into groups, take *notes,* view and *listen to* the video about the mural rut from the Caves of Lescuax. They must write down new vocabulary words that they are unfamiliar with in their notebooks. There will be various dictionaries on hand in their native language if needed
Student Break	10 Minutes	Students have a short relaxation time	Students may get a snack or bring one of their own. Sometimes teacher will bring a special surprise snack… maybe a "cave-man" snack.

Activities	10 Minutes	Independent Practice	After students take notes from watching and listening to video, they can start to draw any one of the images that they admired (people or animals) and write a short sentence about what caught their attention or interested them the most. Then ask them: Would any of these images help them to express their personalities?
Discussion Groups	10 Minutes	Closing/ Student Reflection/ Real Life Connections	Students have small group discussions regarding their reflections and begin research on examples of self-expressive art from the murals of the Caves of Lescaux. They must make a small drawing as if they were living in a cave and depict themselves as a cave dweller. Write a sentence on how modem man depicts murals today as a real life connection.

Differentiated Instruction	Beyond	Differentiated Instruction	Students can make interdisciplinary connections by exploring the life and times of prehistoric cave people This will be the first art history period of six in which students will depict themselves as cave people of that time. Vincent Van Gough and Frida Kahlo are *some* of the artists that are known best for their interesting self-portraits. Students will learn to depict them- selves in six different periods of art history. Students can also choose to make a drawing of Frida Kahlo as a cave lady. They can create self-portraits from the perspective of other people: perhaps from a classmate or as an important historical figure.
Materials	—	—	Personal notebook and art sup- plies such as drawing pencils and art paper as needed and writing materials
Assessment Tools:	—	—	Group World, Demonstration of Skill, Creative Endeavors & Presentation

Course Reading: "Part I The Framework "& "Prut II Strategies" pages 1-17

EDUCATIONAL STANDARDS ADDRESSED: WIDA ELD Standards: Standard 1: Social & Instructional Language: Informed Decisions College & Career WIDA: ELD Standard 2: The Language of Language Arts

WIDA *'s 2012 Amplification of the English Language Development Standard, Kindergarten-Grade 12* ("WIDA ELD Standards") is owned by the Board of Regents of the University of Wisconsin System on behalf of the WIDA Consortium. O 2012 Board of Regents of the University of Wisconsin System, on behalf of the WIDA Consortium-www.wida. us.

CONNECTION: *Common Core Reading Standards for Informational Texts, Integration of Knowledge and Ideas #F.'* Integrate and Evaluate multiple sources of information presented in different media or formats (e.g. visually, quantitatively) as well as in words in order to address a question or solve a problem.

NATIONAL STANDARDS FOR ARTS EDUCATION: The standards outline what every K-12 student should know and be able to do in the arts. The standards were developed by the Consortium of National Arts Education Association

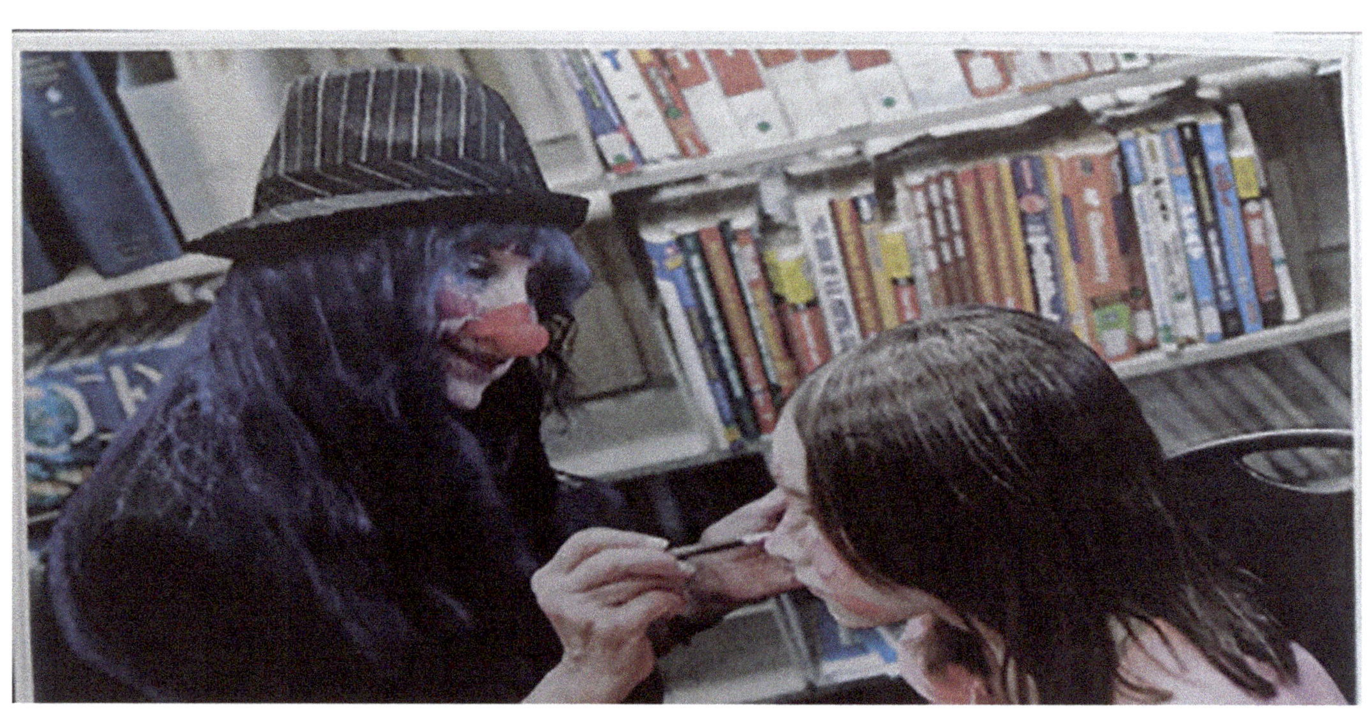

GRADE 9-12 VISUAL ARTS STANDARD 1: Understanding and applying media, techniques, and process

GRADE 9-12 VISUAL ARTS 3TANDARH 2: Using knowledge of structures and functions

GRADE 9-12 VISUAL ARTS STANDARD 3: Choosing and evaluating a range of subject matter, symbols, and ideas

GRADE 9-12 VISUAL ARTS STANDARD 4: Understanding the visual arts in relation to history and cultures

GRADE 9-12 VISUAL ARTS STANDARD **5**: Reflecting upon and assessing the characteristics and merits of their work and the work of others

GRADE 9-12 VISUAL ARTS STANDARD 6: Malting connections between visual arts and other disciplines

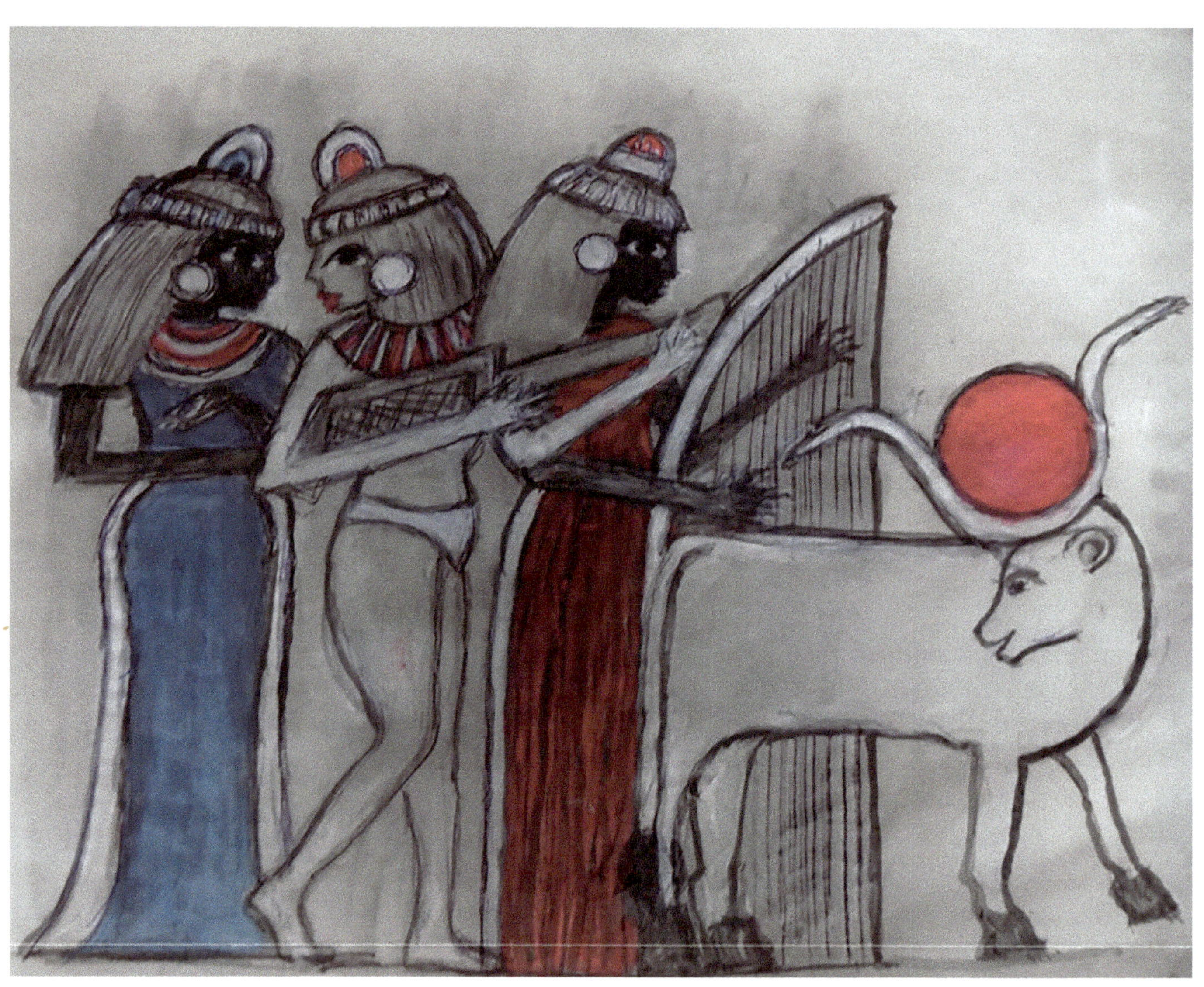

LESSON PLAN FOR DAY TWO

1.5 HOURS - 90 MINUTES

NAME OF LESSON: Exploring Ancient Egyptian Art and Culture

GRADE LEVEL: Junior College:

SUBJECT: ESL/Art

COURSE OVERVIEW: Self-Portraits Through Ages of Art History is a course that will provide context for English language Learners to experience self-discovery through the venue of art. When art is incorporated into the ESL core curriculum it enhances students' engagement and comprehension, increases whole-brain activity, and challenges overall growth in the learning process.

COURSE OBJECTIVES: Upon completion of this course the student will be able to identify and recognize six periods of art history, learn new vocabulary, and be able to *express* their feelings through the written word, oral discussions, and experience self-discovery through the venue of art. They can make interdisciplinary connections as they explore the life and times of *sell* portrait artists and create their own self-portrait from the perspective of different time periods and artists. Students can create an artistic work that is entirely unique and gain a sense of accomplishment.

Review of course overview, syllabus and assignments	10 Minutes	Instructional Input	Teacher will introduce students to the world of Egyptian art and culture. She will demonstrate and describe how she created the artwork that depicts her version of the Egyptian world.
Students begin research on Egyptian art and culture as they examine hand-outs, books, and all relevant materials	20 Minutes	Guided Practice	Students will view handouts and peruse materials describing Egyptian art and culture. Teacher will model reading aloud. Students follow by breaking up into groups and taking turns reading aloud. They can choose pair-share reading and choral reading which teacher will explain.
Clips and Excerpts from the final tomb scene from the Opera Aida	20 Minutes	Vocabulary: Tomb, sarcophagus, pharaoh,	Students observe, listen, take notes and thinly about some of the viewed opera personalities they would like to depict that might describe their personalities. What character caught their attention the most and what did they see in any of the characters that they saw in themselves?
Student Break	10 Minutes	Students have a short relaxation time	Students may get a snack or bring one of their own. Sometimes teacher might bring a special snack (maybe an Egyptian snack.)

Activities and Materials: Special paper or cloth material to depict mu- rals and watercolor and colored paint sets will be provided	15 Minutes	Independent Practice	Students must put their thoughts together about what sentence they will write about their self-portrait character. Today they will learn how to paint by utilizing colored paint sets. Teacher will explain that painting is drawing in color and demonstrates technique. Students begin to create representations of themselves or favorite character in water- colors on special paper or cloth and write a short sentence that expresses their feelings and emotions. They may start their *drawings.*
Discussion Groups	15 Minutes	Closing/ Student Reflection/ Real Life Connections	Students reflect upon their thoughts and writings about Egyptian life, art, and culture. Students can have Socratic questioning on how life and art in Egypt differs today.
Assessment Tools: Art Rubric Guide	—	—	Creative Endeavors (of Group & Individual Work), Presentation, Demonstration of Skill, Active Participation
Differentiated Instruction			Students could enact a scene as Egyptians in a daily life situation such as going to the market and buying necessary items.

Course Reading: "Dramatic Arts" pages 19-37

EDUCATIONAL STANDARDS ADDRESSED: WIDA ELD Standards: Standard 1: Social & Instructional Language: Informed Decisions College & Career WIDA: ELD Standard 2: The Language of Language Arts

WIDA 's 2012 *Amplification of the English Language Development Standards, Kindergarten-Grab 12* ("WIDA ELD Standards") is owned by the Board of Regents of the University of Wisconsin System on behalf of the WIDA Consortium. O 2012 Board of Regents of the University of Wisconsin System, on behalf of the WIDA Consortium-www.wida.us.

CONNECTION: *Common Core Reading Standard for Informational **Texts,** Integration of Knowledge and Ideas* #7: Integrate and Evaluate multiple sources of information presented in different media or formats (e.g. visually, quantitatively) as well as in words in order to address a question or solve a problem.

NATIONAL STANDARDS POR ARTS EDUCATION: The standards outline what every K-12 student should know and be able to do in the arts. The standards were developed by the Consortium of National Arts Education Association

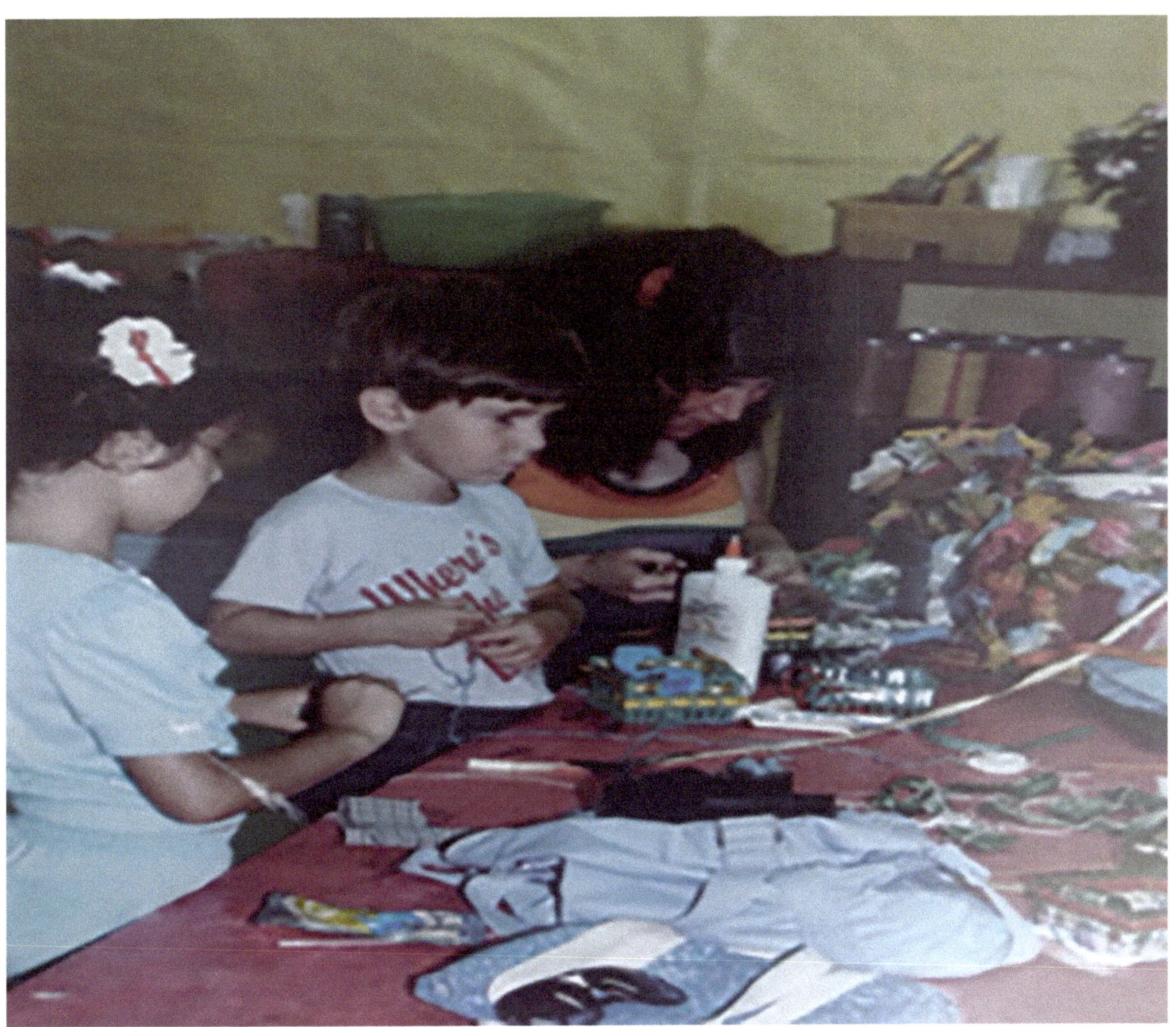

GRADE 9-12 VISUAL ARTS STANDARD 1: Understanding and applying media, techniques, and processes

GRADE 9-12 VISUAL ARTS STANDARD 2: Using knowledge of structures and functions

GRADE 9-12 VISUAL ARTS STANDARD 3: Choosing and evaluating a range of subject matter, symbols, and ideas

GRADE 9-12 VISUAL ARTS STANDARD 4: Understanding the visual arts in relation to history and cultures

GRADE P-12 VISUAL ARTS STANDARD 5: Reflecting upon and assessing the characteristics and merits of their work and the work of others

GRADE 9-12 VISUAL ARTS STANDARD 6: Making connections between visual arts and other disciplines

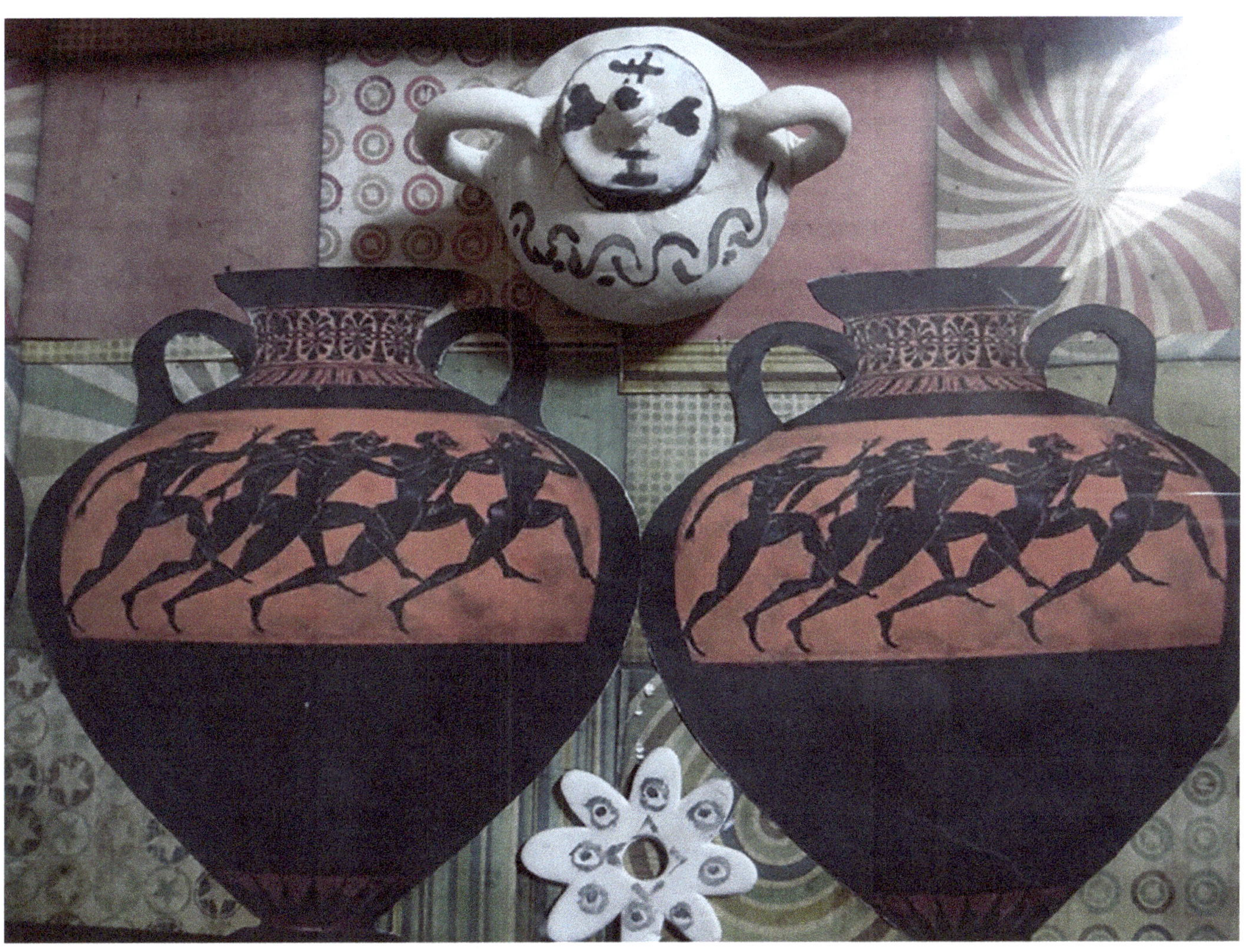

LESSON PLAN FOR DAY THREE
1.5 HOURS - 90 MINUTES

NAME OF LESSON: Exploring The World of Greek Art

GRADE LEYEL: Junior College

SUBJECT: ESL/Art

COURSE OVERVIEW: Self-Portraits Through Ages of Art History is a course that will provide context for English language Learners to experience self-discovery through the venue of art. When art is incorporated into the ESL core curriculum it enhances students' engagement and comprehension, increases whole-brain activity, and challenges overall growth in the learning process.

COURSE OBJECTIVES: Upon completion of this course the student will be able to identify and recognize six periods of arc history, learn new vocabulary, and be able to express their feelings through the written word, oral discussions, and experience self-discovery through the venue of art. Explanations of each art period and culture will follow course format. Students can make interdisciplinary connections as they explore the life and times of self-portrait artists and create their own self-portrait from the perspective of different time periods and artists. Students can create an artistic work that *is* entirely unique and gain a sense of accomplishment.

Introduction to Lesson	10 Minutes	Instructional Input	Teacher will give short introduction to students on Greek art history and have pictures and materials and website sources to share with students. Teacher will bring a Greek style mixed media artwork entitled "Daedalus' Delta" to share with students. Teacher will share info on Ancient Greek artists and artisans who have produced some of the most impressive works of art. Students will explore and discover how Greert architecture and sculpture still retain the highest standards of excellence all over the world and learn how Greek artisans have contributed special painting techniques.
Group Activities	20 Minutes	Guided Practice	Students will discuss research findings and build upon previous knowledge of what they already know about Greek art. Following the discussion students will describe and write short sentences describing their findings on Fayum Mummy portraits and Hellenistic and Greek genre style painting.

Video of Greek Fayum Mummy style, Hellenistic, and genre paintings	10 Minutes	Vocabulary: Genre painting, landscape painting, Fayum Mummy portraits, linear perspective, encaustic, tempera	Students write down new vocabulary words. After researching the two styles, students can choose to engage in Total Response Activities as they re- enact roles of various Greek painters who are extolling the virtues of their preferred painting styles. All students will get to voice their opinions and preferences as well as switch roles.
Student Break	10 Minutes	Students have a short relaxation time	Students may get a snack or bring one of their own. Teacher might bring Greek figs or grape-leaf snack as an appreciation of Greek culinary culture.
Activities	25 Minutes	Independent Practice	Teacher will describe and give information about each type of painting style. Students choose their favorite style in which to depict themselves. The choice will be between the Fayum Mummy style and the Hellenistic style. Various hand- *outs* and pictures of Greek art will be available. After students depict themselves in the preferred painting style they will write short sentences which describe what they liked about that style and how it fits their particular personality.
Discussion Groups	15 Minutes	Closing/Student Reflection/ Real Life Connections	Students have a discussion in groups of four. Leader of group can give a short oral report regarding students' reflections on how Greek sculpture and architecture still influence and impact our modem world today.

Differentiated Instruction	Beyond	Differentiated Instruction	Students may choose to make a small Greek pottery out of sculpey. Teacher will demonstrate and model how to knead and form sculpey into small Greek vase shapes. Instructor will take vases home and bake them accordingly. When instructor brings them back the class can paint Greek geometric designs of their choice on them
Materials: pictures of Greek Hellenistic Genre paintings, sculpey and art and writing paper as needed.	--	--	Students will learn how to manipulate sculpey in order to form Greek vase shapes.
Assessment Tools: Art Rubric	--	—	Group Work, Demonstration Creative Endeavors & Presentation of Skill,

Course Reading: "Creative Writing Pages 41-52

EDUCATIONAL STANDARDS ADDRESSED: IDA ELD Standards: Standard 1: Social & Instructional Language: Informed Decisions College & Career WI DA: ELD Standard 2: The Language of Language Arts

WIDA 's 2012 *Amplification of the English Language Development Standards, Kindergarten -Grade 12* ("WIDA ELD Standards") is owned by the Board of Regents of the University of Wisconsin System on behalf of the WIDA Consortium. fi 2012 Board of Regents of the University of Wisconsin System, on behalf of the WJDA Consortium-wvw.wida.us.

CONNECTION: *Common Core Reading Standards for Informational Texts, Integration of Knowledge and Idea* #Y: Integrate and Evaluate multiple sources of information presented in different media or formats (e.g. visually, quantitatively) as well as in words in order to address a question or solve a problem.

NATIONAL STANDARDS FOR ARTS EDUCATION: The standards outline what every K-12 student should know and be able to do in the arts. The standards were developed by the Consortium of National Arts Education Association

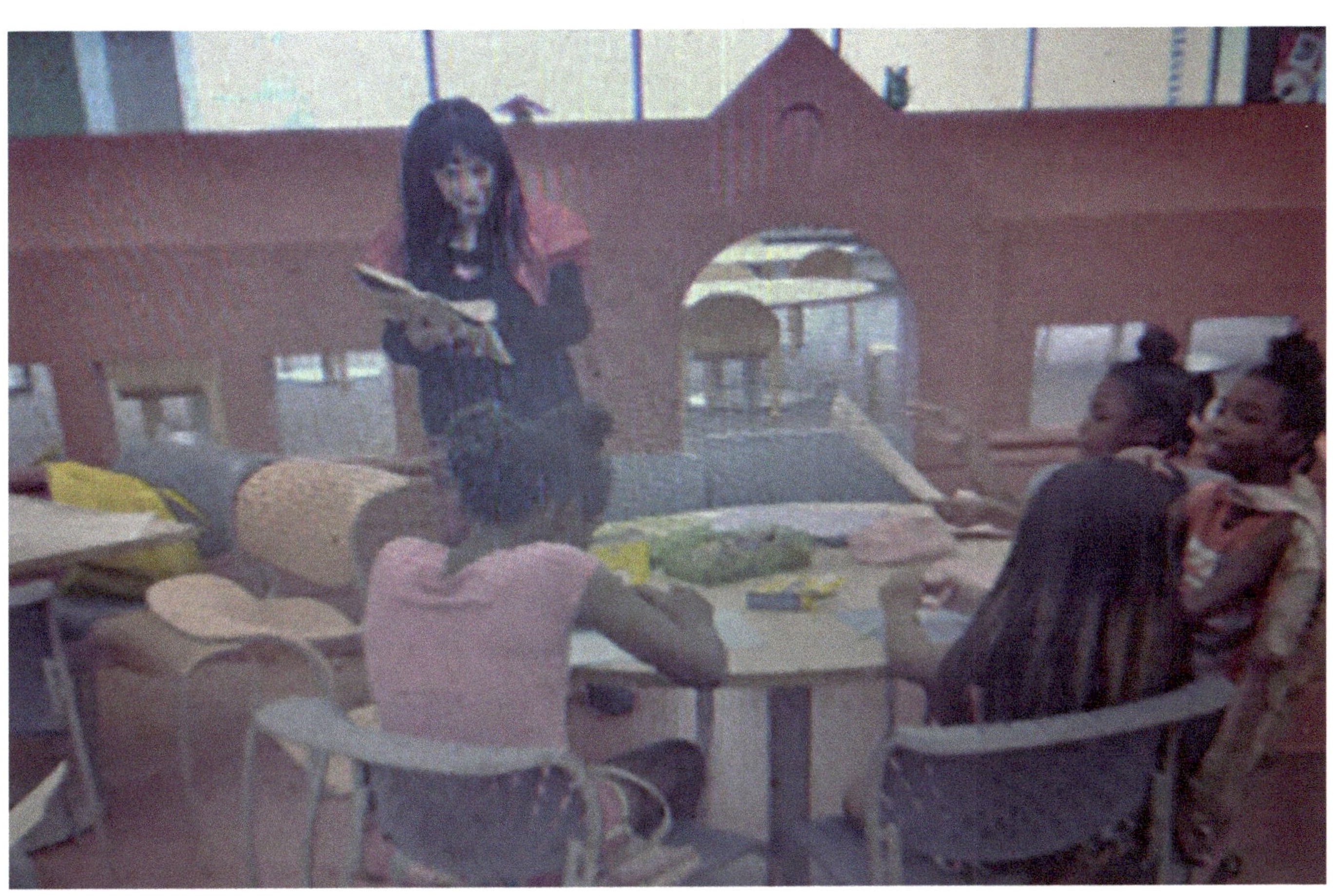

GRADE 9-12 VISUAL ARTS STANDARD 1: Understanding and applying media, techniques, and processes

GRADE 9-12 VISUAL ARTS STANDARD 2: Using knowledge of structures and functions

GRADE 9-12 VISUAL ARTS STANDARD 3: Choosing and evaluating a range of subject matter, symbols, and ideas

GRADE 9-12 VISUAL ARTS STANDARD 4: Understanding the visual arts in relation to history and cultures

GRADE 9-12 VISUAL ARTS STANDARD 5: Reflecting upon and assessing the characteristics and merits of their works and the work of others

GRADE 9-12 VISUAL ARTS STANDARD 6: Making connections between visual arts and other disciplines

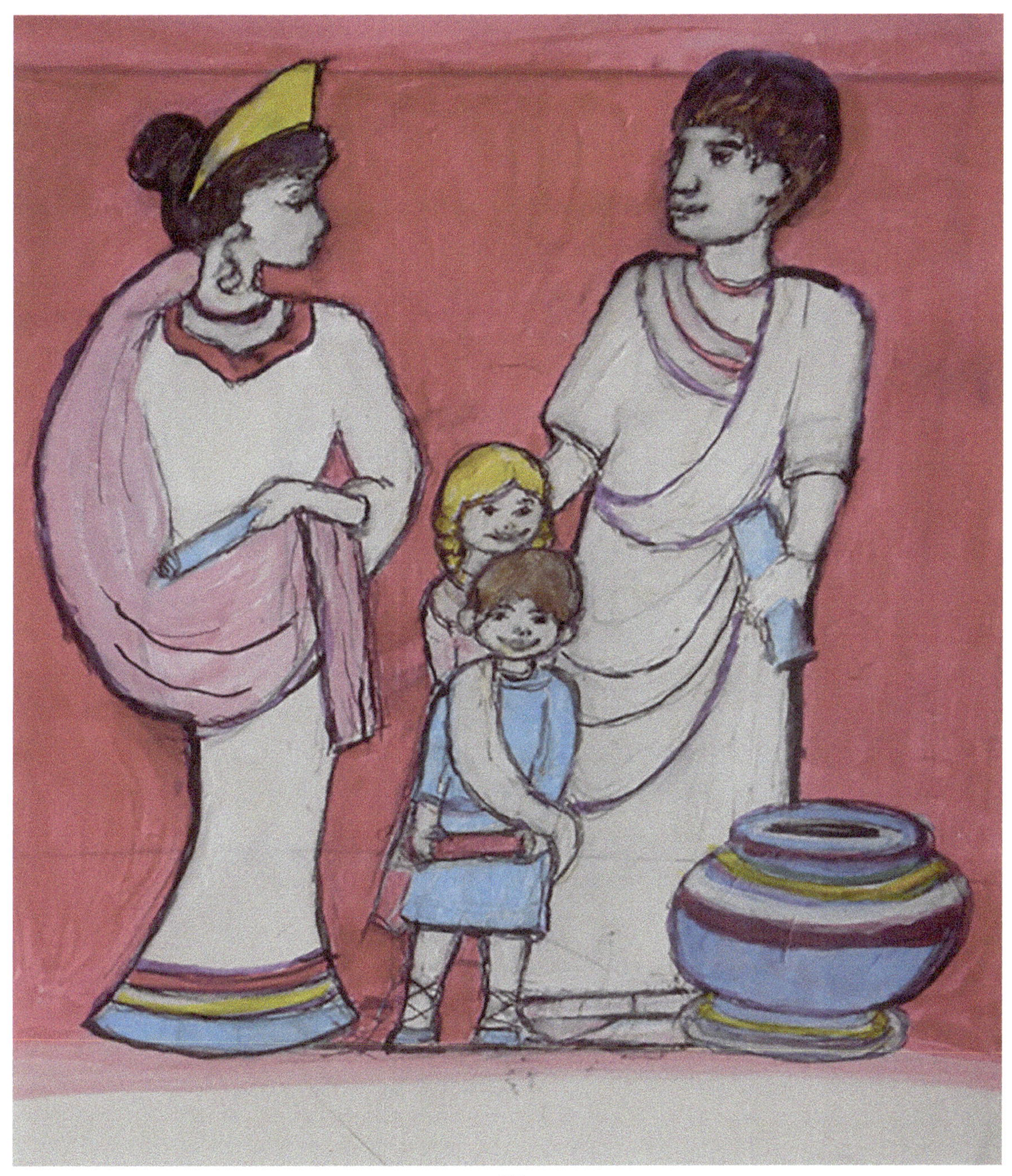

LESSON PLAN FOR DAY FOUR

1.5 HOURS -90 MINUTES

NAME OF LESSON: Exploring The World of Roman Art and Fresco

GRADE LEVEL: Junior College

SUBJECT: ESL/Art

COURSE OVERVIEW: Self-Portraits Through Ages of Alt History is a course that will provide context for English language Learners to experience self-discovery through the venue of art. When art is incorporated into the ESL core curriculum it enhances students' engagement and comprehension, increases whole-brain activity, and challenges overall growth in the learning process.

COURSE OBJECTIVES: Upon completion of this course the student will be able to identify and recognize six periods of art history, learn new vocabulary, and be able to express their feelings through the written word, oral discussions, and experience self-discovery through the venue of art. Explanations of each art period and culture will follow course format. Students can matte interdisciplinary connections as they explore the life and times of self-portrait artists and create their own self-portrait from the perspective of different time periods and artists. Students can create an artistic work that is entirely unique and gain a sense of accomplishment.

Introduction to Lesson	10 Minutes	Instructional Input	Teacher will give short introduction to students on Roman art history and explanation how mural fresco painting began. The focus of this lesson will be viewing and analyzing examples of fresco and at seco self-portrait art from ancient the city of Pompei in Rome.
Group Activities	20 Minutes	Guided Practice	Many examples of Roman self- portraits still exist today in beautifully painted murals that have been preserved and restored. Students will begin research and discussions on Roman fresco styles of portrait paintings. Students will have discussions regarding their research findings and build upon their previous knowledge.
Clips of Pompeii Murals and Mosaics	20 Minutes	Vocabulary: Mural paintings, al fresco, al seco, funerary sculp- ture, life style statues, La Tene style, Roman- Celtic art, friezes	Teacher demonstrates and models to students what similarities and differences are and explains by demonstrating the comparison and contrast between the al seco and al fresco styles of painting. Students will write their own short para- graphs in conclusion about which style they refer and why
Student Break	10 Minutes	Students have a short relaxation time	Students may get a snack or bring one of their own. Sometimes teacher will surprise them and bring a special snacks.

Activities	15 Minutes	Independent Practice	Students will create drawings in colored pencils of themselves and paint themselves in the style of Roman fresco art they prefer. They can also choose to work in the medium of clay and construct their own small Roman style frieze type of sculpture.
Discussion Groups Podcast or virtual reality trip to a famous art museum	15 Minutes	Closing/Student Reflection/ Real Life Connections	Students may have a discussion in groups of four. The Leader or spokesperson in each group can give a short oral report regarding all of the students' reflections.
Differentiated Instruction	Beyond	Differentiated Instruction	Students could imagine that they are artists back in ancient Rome. They can inquire among *themselves* which self- portrait style of portrait they would prefer to be painted in... al secco or at *fresco* and then execute their painting in the painting style of their choice.
Materials	—	—	Art supplies such as lightweight clay, drawing pencils, watercolors and acrylics, and art paper as needed and writing materials
Assessment Tools:			Group World, Demonstration of Skill, Creative Endeavors & Presentation. The process of artistic creating and active involvement in creating is considered to be more important than the quality of the final product. (i.e. discovery, inquiry, analysis, and expression *is* what counts.)

Course Reading: "Music and Rhythm" Pages 55-66

EDUCATIONAL STANDARDS ADDRESSED: WIDA ELD Standards: Standard 1: Social & Instructional Language: Informed Decisions College & Career IDA: ELD Standard 2: The Language of Language Arts

WIDA *'s* 2012 *Amplification of the English Language Development Standards, Kindergarten-trade 12* ("WJDA ELD Standards") is owned by the Board of Regents of the University of Wisconsin System on behalf of the WIDA Consortium. fi 2012 Board of Regents of the University of Wisconsin System, on behalf of the WIDA Consortium-www.wida.us.

CONNECTION: *Common More Reading Standards or Informational Texts, Integration of Knowledge and Ideas #7:'* Integrate and Evaluate multiple sources of information presented in different media or formats (e.g. visually, quantitatively) as well as in words in order to address a question or solve a problem.

NATIONAL STANDARDS FOR ARTS EDUCATION: The standards outline what every K-12 student should know and be able to do in the arts. The standards were developed by the Consortium of National Arts Education Association

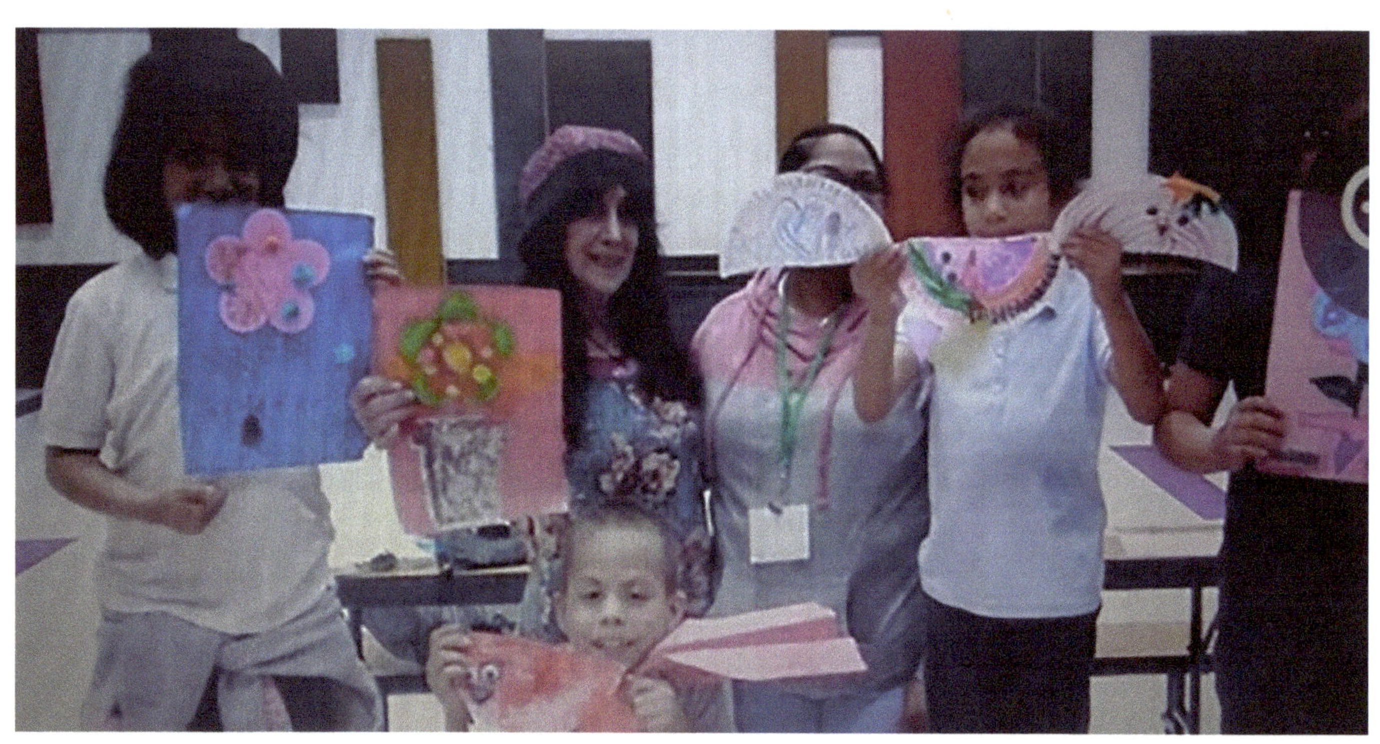

GRADE 9-12 VISUAL ARTS STANDARD 1: Understanding and applying media, techniques, and processes

GRADE 9-12 VISUAL ARTS STANDARD 2: Using knowledge of structures and functions

GRADE 9-12 VISUAL ARTS STANDARD 3: Choosing and evaluating a range of subject matter, symbols, and ideas

GRADE 9-12 VISUAL ARTS STANDARD 4: Understanding the visual arts in relation to history and cultures

GRADE 9-12 VISUAL ARTS STANDARD 5: Reflecting upon and assessing the characteristics and merits of their work and the work of others

GRADE 9-12 VISUAL ARTS STANDARD 6: Making connections between visual arts and other disciplines

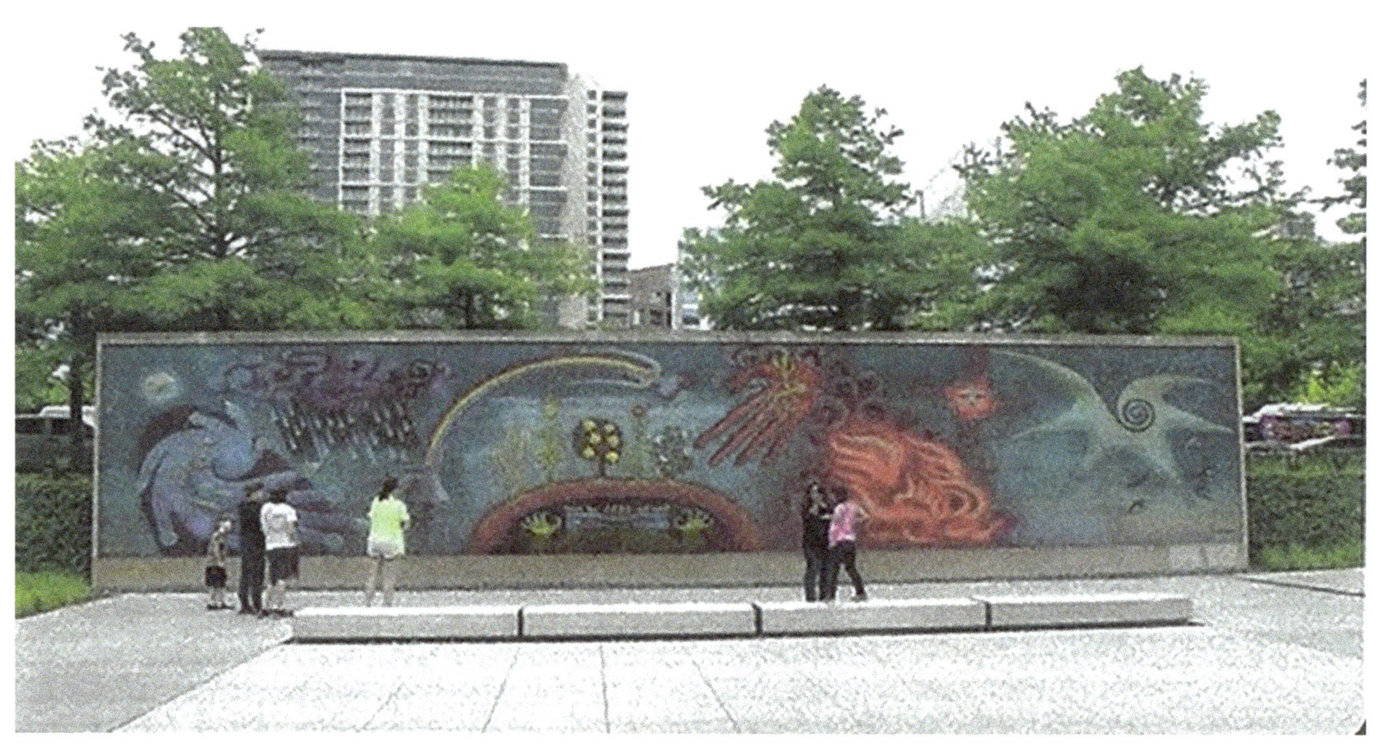

LESSON PLAN FOR DAY FIVE

1.5 HOURS - 90 MINUTES

NAME OF LESSON: Trip To Dallas Museum of Art/DMA or Virtual Reality Tour of Versailles Museum In Paris

GRADE LEVEL: Junior College

SUBJECT: SSL/Art

COURSE OVERVIEW: Self-Portraits Through Ages of Art History *is* a course that will provide context for English language Learners to experience self-discovery through the venue of art. When art is incorporated into the ESL core curriculum it enhances students' engagement and comprehension, increases whole-brain activity, and challenges overall growth in the learning process.

COURSE OBJECTIVES: Upon completion of this course the student will be able to identify and recognize six periods of art history learn new vocabulary, and be able to express their feelings through the written word, oral discussions, and experience self-discovery through the venue of art. They can make interdisciplinary connections as they explore the life and times of self-portrait artists and create their own self-portrait from the perspective of different time periods and artists. Students can create an artistic work that is entirely unique and gain a sense of accomplishment.

Introduction to Visit to DMA or computer/video Virtual Reality Tour of the Art Museum of Versailles	10 Minutes	Instructional Input	Teacher and students will meet either at the DMA or if not possible meet in the classroom for a virtual reality tour of the art from the Museum of Versailles in Paris, France. The Virtual Reality Tour will be treated in the same manner as if we were in Versailles viewing the art and concentrating on the six historical studied art periods. Instructor and students will view all six ages of art history in our course, but if time permits, we can explore more, if not all of the art at the DMA. Students and teachers can bring sketchpads (if they desire) and take notes as they write down observations and make quick sketches. Students should make observations and take notes about what art impressed them the most and what art might have dis- pleased them. Writing down observations helps strengthen students' critical thinking abilities.
Group Activities	30 Minutes	Guided Tour	We may or may not have a guided tour. As a student group we might be able to get a discounted group rate and be able to have a guided tour by a trained docent who is extremely knowledgeable about all the art at the DMA; otherwise we will create our own guided tour.

Teacher/Student Interactions	10 Minutes	Vocabulary: Whatever new words students discover and wish to record in their notebooks as they explore the art	Teacher always mentors and models good public behavior when traveling with the students.
Cafe	20 Minutes	Students and teacher may stop off at the DMA Cafe for a treat	Students may rake a vote to *see* if the group would like to visit the DMA Cafe for some cafe food and see the beautiful glass artwork of Chalullv.
DMA	10 Minutes	Closing/Student Reflection/ Real Life Connections	Students can make observations and take notes of all the different mediums that are on display that have been employed by different artists and artisans. Students may have a discussion later when class meets again based upon their observational notes about their likes and dislikes and artist's usage of the different kinds of art media.
Differentiated Instruction	Beyond	Differentiated Instruction	Daily EFL Restaurant TPR Role-Play "Odaiba Coffee Shop." Students could imagine that they are docents in the museum and could classify and draw up time-lines of all the art history periods.
Materials	-	Sketch pads and notebooks	
Assessment Tools:			Observations and *comments* in notebooks

No Course Reading

EDUCATIONAL STANDARDS ADDRESSED: WIDA ELD Standards: Standard 1: Social & Instructional Language: Informed Decisions College R Career WIDA: ELD Standard 2: The Language of Language Arts

WIDA 's 2012 *Amplification of the English Language Development Standards, Kindergarten-Grade 12* ("WIDA ELD Standards") is owned by the Board of Regents of the University of Wisconsin System on behalf of the WADA Consortium. © 2012 Board of Regents of the University of Wisconsin System, on behalf of the WIDA Consortium-www.wida.us.

CONNECTION: *Common Core Reading Standards for Informational Texts, Integration of Knowledge and Ideas* #7: Integrate and Evaluate multiple sources of information presented in different media or formats (e.g. visually, quantitatively) as well as in words in order to address a question or solve a problem.

NATIONAL STANDARDS FOR ARTS EDUCATION: The standards outline what every K-12 student should know and be able to do in the arts. The standards were developed by the Consortium of National Arts Education Association

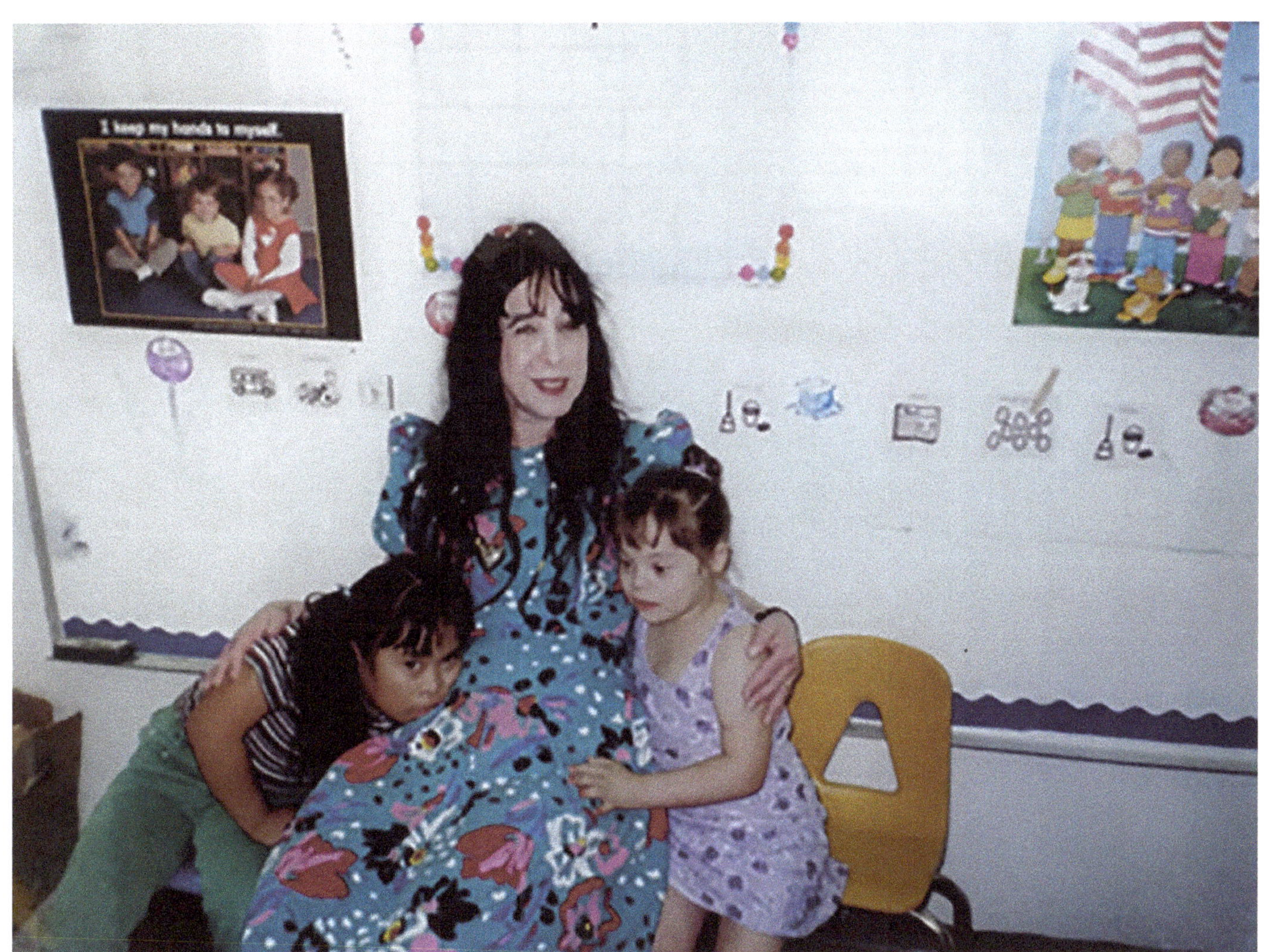

I keep my hands to myself.

GRADE 9-12 VISUAL ARTS STANDARD 1: Understanding and applying media, techniques, and processes

GRADE 9-12 VISUAL ARTS STANDARD 2: Using knowledge of structures and functions

GRADE 9-12 VISUAL ARTS STANDARD 3: Choosing and evaluating a range of subject matter, symbols, and ideas

GRADE 9-12 VISUAL ARTS STANDARD 4: Understanding the visual arts in relation to history and cultures

GRADE 9-12 VISUAL ARTS STANDARD 5: Reflecting upon and assessing the characteristics and merits of their work and the work of others

GRADE 9-12 VISUAL ARTS STANDARD 6: Making connections between visual arts and other disciplines

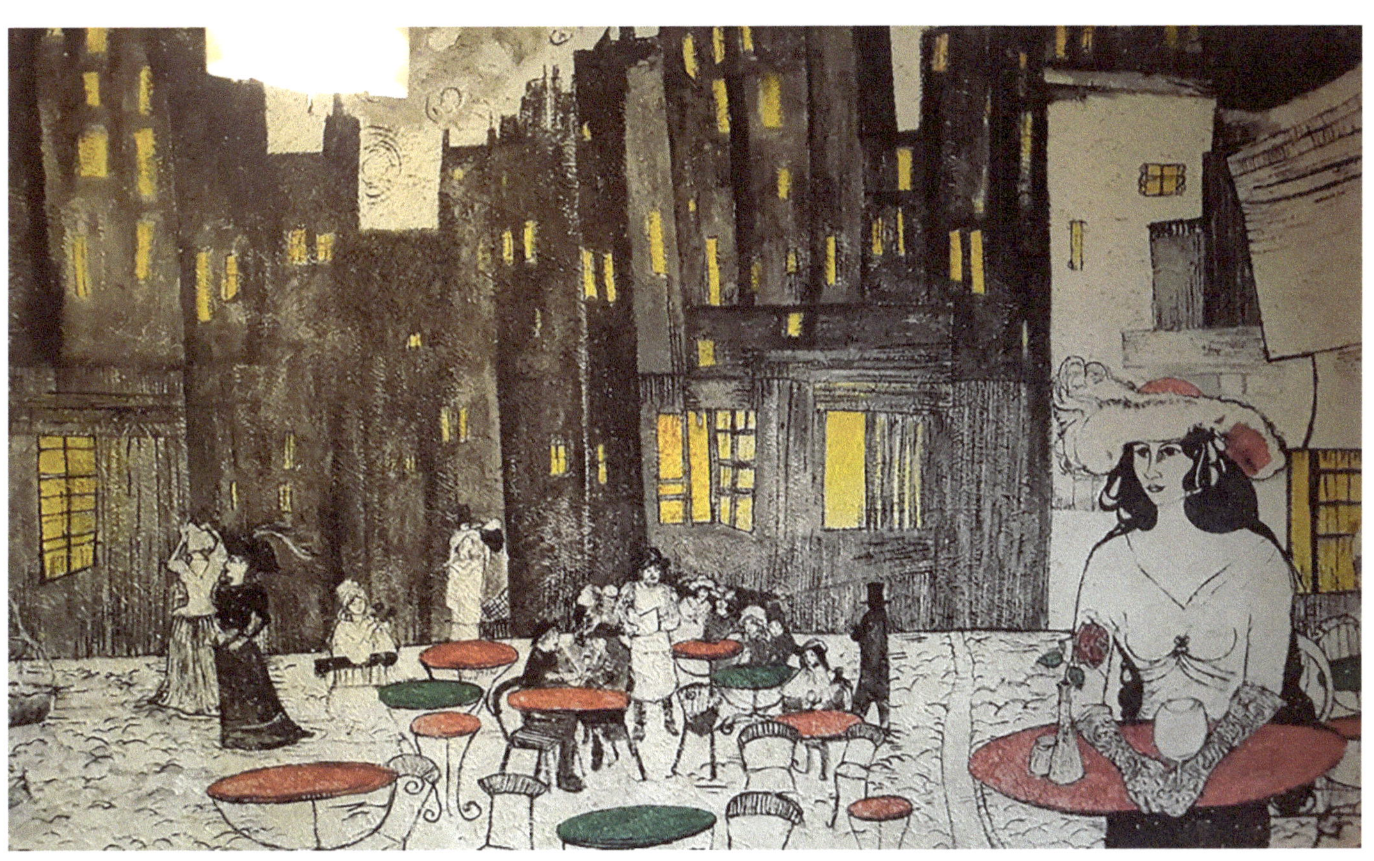

LESSON PLAN FOR DAY SIX
1.5 HOURS - 90 MINUTES

NAME OF LESSON: Exploring The Art of The Impressionists

GRADE LEVEL: Junior College:

SUBJECT: ESL/Art

COURSE OVERVIEW: Self-Portraits Through Ages of Art History is a course that will provide context for English language Learners to experience self-discovery through the venue of art. then art is incorporated into the ESL core curriculum it enhances students' engagement and comprehension, increases whole-brain activity, and challenges overall growth in the learning process.

COURSE OBJECTIVES: Upon completion of this course the student will be able to identify and recognize six periods of art history, learn new vocabulary, and be able to express their feelings through the written word, oral discussions, and experience self-discovery through the venue of art. They can make interdisciplinary connections as they explore the life and times of self portrait artists and create their own self-portrait from the perspective of different time periods and artists. Students can create an artistic work that is entirely unique and gain a sense of accomplishment.

Introduction to Lesson	10 Minutes	Instructional Input	Teacher will give short introduction to stu- dents on the Impressionist and Expressionist movement and discuss some of be most striking self-portrait artist such as Vincent Van Gogh, Auguste Renoir, and Paul Gauguin.
Videos and Materials on Impressionism and Expressionism About. com Video: What Is Impressionism?	20 Minutes	Guided Practice	While teacher shows videos students will take notes and will be able to list all the Impressionist and Expressionist painters and write a sentence about what each rutist was known for in their painting style. Teacher will assist in answering questions and helping students choose other research materials. The class will focus their attention on the rutists Auguste Renoir; Paul Gauguin, and Vincent Van Gogh.
Randall's ESL Cyber Listening Lab ESL	20 Minutes	Vocabulary: Impressionism, fau- vism. Expressionism,	Students engage in listening and answering activities as they learn to use their new vocabulary words in multiple situations. Randall's ESL Cyber Listening Lab has several good listening and response activity opportunities.
Student Break	10 Minutes	Students have a short relaxation time	Students may get a snack or bring one of their own. Sometimes teacher will surprise them and bring a special snack

Activities	15 Minutes	Independent Practice	Students will use colored pastels and magic markers to draw their artistic creations on rut paper in the style of Vincent Van Gogh or Paul Gaugin. Students will write a short summary of what they learned about Impressionism and Expressionism and why they liked or disliked this style and express themselves through the written word if any of the characters expressed any aspect of their own personalities. They can use their new vocabulary to connect to new thoughts.
Discussion Groups	15 Minutes	Closing/Student Reflection/ Real Life Connections	Students may engage in discussions in groups of three or four or corporately. If they sit in a semi-circle they might embrace choral reading. Each group could alternate *between* choral readings and round robin readings as they share their thoughts and opinions about the history and importance of the movement into their work.
Differentiated Instruction	Beyond	Differentiated Instruction	Students could participate in a Total Physical Response activity by putting on a short play that they envisioned and wrote themselves about the short life of Vincent Van Gogh. They could take turns acting out these roles in the misunderstanding between Gaugin and Van Gogh.
Materials		—	Art supplies today will include art paper and a rich set of pastels and colored markers.

Assessment Tools:	—		Group Work, Demonstration of Skill, Creative Endeavors & Presentation. The process of artistic creating and active involvement in creating is counted as more important than the quality of the final product. (i.e. discovery, inquiry, analysis, and expression)

Course Reading: "Dance and Movement" Pages 68-77

EDUCATIONAL STANDARDS ADDRESSED: WIDA ELD Standards: Standard 1: Social & Instructional Language: Informed Decisions College & Career WIDA: ELD Standard 2: The Language of Language Arts

WIDA 's 2012 *Amplification of the English Language Development Standards, Kindergarten-trade 12* ("WIDA ELD Standards") is owned by the Board of Regents of the University of Wisconsin System on behalf of the WIDA Consortium. O 2012 Board of Regents of the University of Wisconsin System, on behalf of the WIDA Consortium-www.wida.us.

CONNECTION: *Common Core Reading Standards for Informational Texts, Integration of Knowledge* n d *Ideas* #7; Integrate and Evaluate multiple sources of information presented in different media or formats (e.g. visually, quantitatively) as well as in words in order to address a question or solve a problem.

NATIONAL STANDARDS FOR ARTS EDUCATION: The standards outline what every K-12 student should know and be able to do in the arts. The standards were developed by the Consortium of National Arts Education Association

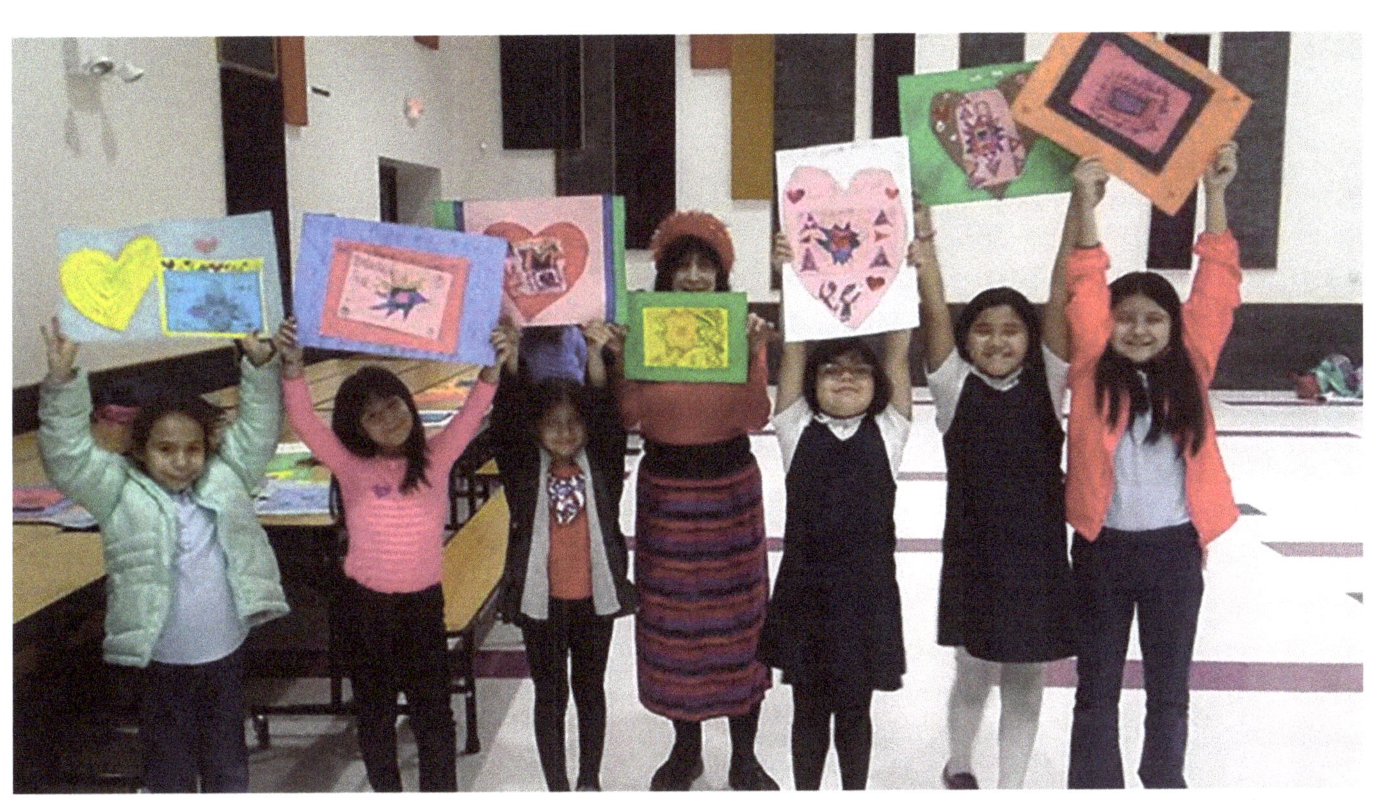

GRADE 9-12 VISUAL ARTS STANDARD 1: Understanding and applying media, techniques, and processes

GRADE 9-12 VISUAL ARTS STANDARD 2: Using knowledge of structures and functions

GRADE 9-12 VISUAL ARTS STANDARD 3: Choosing and evaluating a range of subject matter, symbols, and ideas

GRADE 9-12 VISUAL ARTS STANDARD 4: Understanding the visual arts in relation to history and cultures

GRADE 9-12 VISUAL ARTS STANDARD 5: Reflecting upon and assessing the characteristics and merits of their work and the world of others

GRADE 9-12 VISUAL ARTS STANDARD 6: Making connections between visual arts and other disciplines

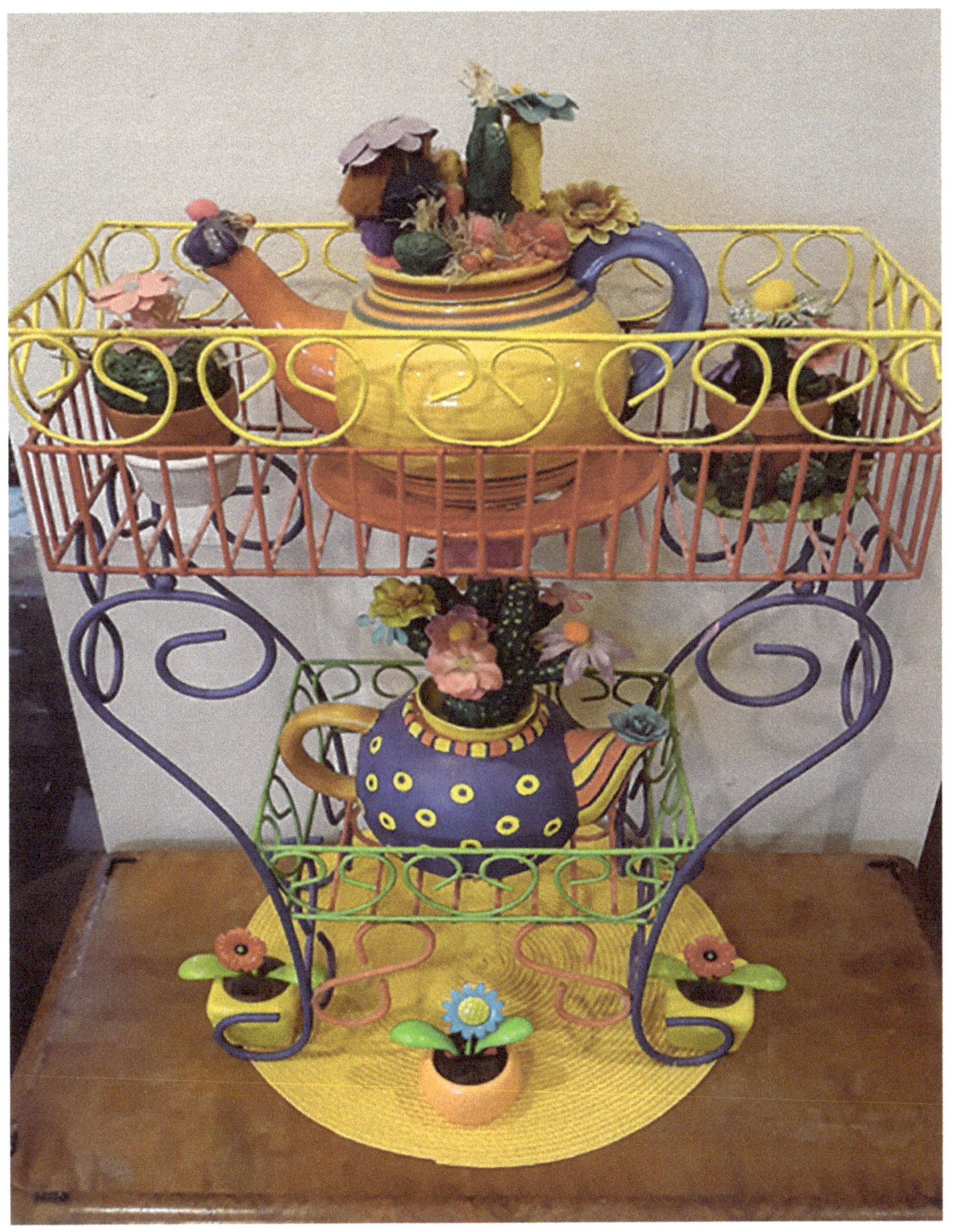

LESSON PLAN FOR DAY SEVEN
1.5 HOURS -90 MINUTES

NAME OF LESSON: Exploring Modem and Contemporary Art

GRADE LEVEL: Junior College

SUBJECT: ESL/Art

COURSE OVERVIEW Self-Portraits Through *Ages* of Art History is a course that will *provide* context for English language Learners to experience self-discovery through the venue of art. When art is incorporated into the ESL core curriculum it enhances students' engagement and comprehension, increases whole-brain activity, and challenges overall growth in the learning process.

COURSE OBJECTIVES: Upon completion of this course students will be able to identify and recognize six periods of art history, learn new vocabulary, and be able to express their feelings through the written word, oral discussions, and experience self-discovery through the venue of art.

LESSON #7: By the end of this lesson students will understand how the works of Henri Matisse and Pablo Picasso developed and still influence the art and culture of today. Students will compare and contrast works of these two artists at different periods of their lives. They can make interdisciplinary connections as they explore the life and times of Matisse and Picasso and create self-portraits by expressing and infusing their personalities into the different time periods of these artists.

Students will be able to make connections between their personal experiences and feelings as a work of art and use their visual analysis skills to verbally describe details. Students will be able to produce their own uniquely created artwork.

Overview of Lesson	10 Minutes	Instructional Input	Teacher will give short synopsis on lives and times of Henri Matisse and Pablo Picasso who helped inspire new artistic movements and will pass out various informative hand-outs.
Videos, clips, and internet websites about Matisse and Picasso	20 Minutes	Guided Practice	Students will take notes about the lives and *times* of Picasso and Matisse while viewing videos and clips. They can engage in pair-share readings from the hand-outs. After watching video, students will review facts about these two artists. They can answer on paper: 1. What country was each artist from? 2. When did Matisse and Picasso begin to paint professionally?
Materials: Videos and clips on Matisse and Picasso Computer: use of internet websites, pieces of wood, found objects, glue, wire	15 Minutes	Vocabulary: Abstract Expressionism, cubism, sculpture, Impressionist, medium, palette, context, surrealism	Students will write down new vocabulary words, record their meanings, and write meaningful sentences that demonstrate their understanding. "This will always be part of their written homework.
Student Break	10 Minutes	Students have short *relax*-ation time	Students may get a snack or bring one of their own. Sometimes teacher may bring a special surprise snack.

Activities -Writing Activity Followed by Art Activity	25 Minutes:	Independent Practice	There are two websites which students can access on the computer which show specific works by Matisse and Picasso. After students access websites they can break into groups of four and work together to write a small para- graph which will consist *of sentences* which: 1. Describe Matisse and Picasso's early works 2. What other artists or movements might have inspired Picasso and Matisse? In conclusion, students must consider and describe what was unique, innovative, or shocking about Matisse and Picasso's paintings.
Computer Internet Access to: Henri Matisse: Woman with a Hat (1905) Pa blo Picasso: Les Demoiselles d'Avignon (1907)	(10 Minutes: writing activity) (13 Minutes for art activity)		Art activity: Each student will construct their own small sculpture out of various wooden pieces and found objects that the teacher has provided and construct it according to their own perception of modern art. Once students have completed assembling their sculptures, they will paint colorful cubistic style designs of their self-portraits directly onto the wooden sculptures either in the style of Matisse or in the style of Picasso (whichever style they feel is closest to their personalities) in bright, vivid colors.
Discussion Groups	15 Minutes	Closing/Student Reflection/ Real Life Connections	Student discussions on understanding how the art of Matisse and Picasso still impacts the modern world of today.

Differentiated fustruction d 'Avig non (1907) Differentiated Art Lesson Plan Based on the Work of Andy Warhol by Stephanie Geider	Extra	Differentiated instruction	Students can look up the work of Marisol Escobar; the French sculptress who is recognized for her innovative modern sculptures which has influenced American Pop Art.

Daily Assignment: Course Reading "Visual Arts" Pages 79-99

EXTRA INTERNET RESOURCES:

Henri Matisse
MoMA: Matisse
http://www.moma.org/collection/browseresults.php?criteria= 0%3AAD%3AE%3A3832&pagenumber
=l&templateid=6&sortorder=!

Metropolitan Museum of Art: Matisse
http://www.metrnuseum.org/toah/hd/mati/hdmati.htm

MoMA: Matisse
http://www.abcgal1ery.com/M/matisse/matisse8.html
http://www.moma.org/co1lection/browse results.php?criteria=0%3AAD %3AE%3A3832 &pagenumb
er=1&templateid=6&sortorder=!

Pablo Picasso
http://www.abcgallery.com/P/picasso/picasso.html

MoMA: Picasso
http://www.moma.org/collection/browseresults.php?criteria=0%3AAD%3AE%3A4609&pagenumber
=1&templateid=!O&sortorder=!

Metropolitan Museum of Art: Picasso
http://www.metrnuseum. org/toah/hd/pica/hdpica.htm

EDUCATIONAL STANDARDS ADDRESSED: WIDA ELD Standards: Standard 1: Social & Instructional Language: Informed Decisions College & Career WIDA: ELD Standard 2: The Language of Language Arts

WIDA 's 2012 *Amplification of the English Language Development Standards, Kindergarten-trade 12* ("WIDA ELD Standards") is owned by the Board of Regents of the University of Wisconsin System on behalf of the WIDA Consortium. O 2012 Board of Regents of the University of Wisconsin System, on behalf of the WIDA Consortium-www.wida.us.

CONNECTION: *Common Core Reading Standard for Informational Texts, Integration of Knowledge and Ideas* #7: Integrate and Evaluate multiple sources of information presented in different media or formats (e.g. visually, quantitatively) as well as in words in order to address a question or solve a problem.

NATIONAL STANDARDS FOR ARTS EDUCATION: The standards outline what every K-12 student should know and be able to do in the arts. The standards were developed by the Consortium of National Arts Education Association

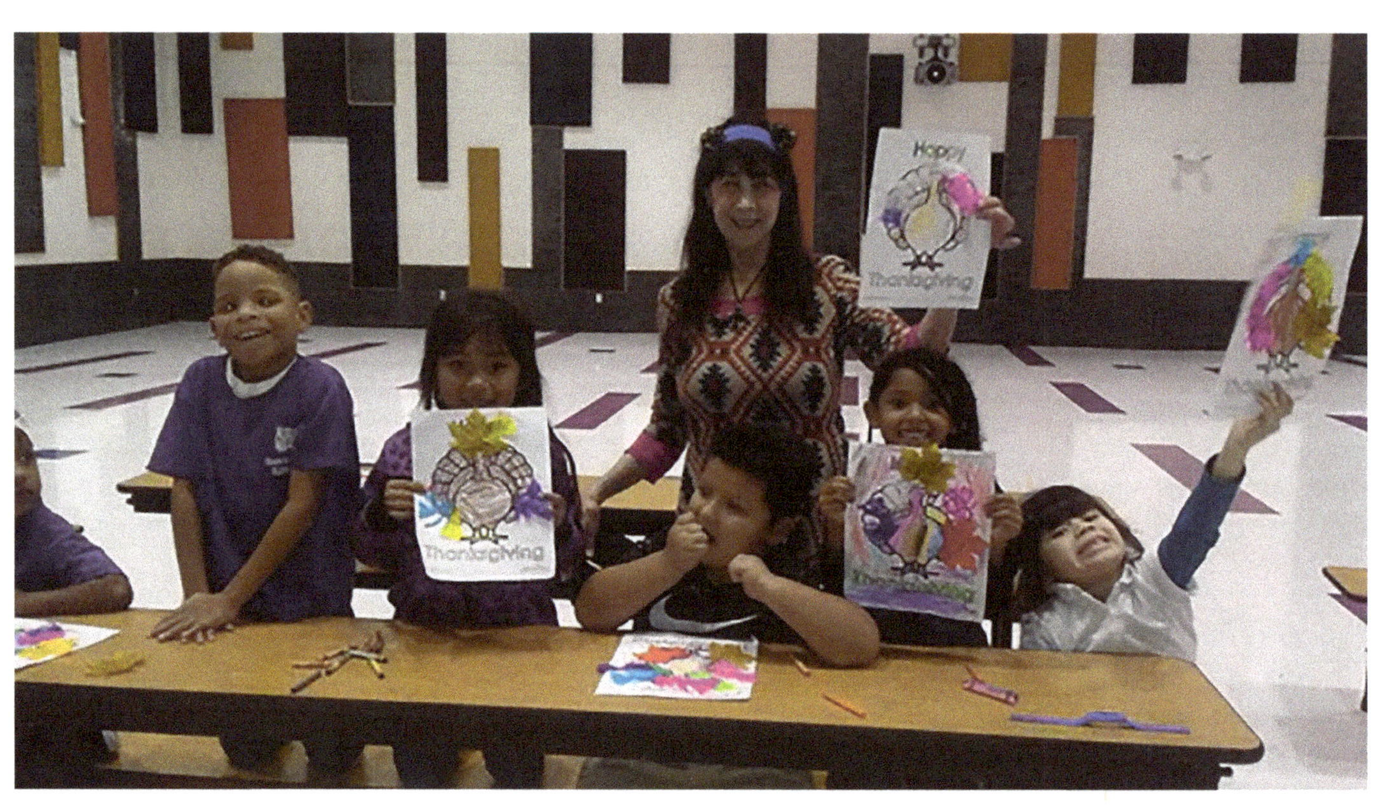

Happy
Thanksgiving
Thanksgiving
Thanksgiving

GRADE 9-12 VISUAL ARTS STANDARD 1: Understanding and applying media, techniques, and processes

GRADE 9-12 VISUAE ARTS STANDARD 2: Using knowledge of structures and functions

GRADE 9-12 USUAL ARTS STANDARD 3: Choosing and evaluating a range of subject matter; symbols, and ideas

GRADE 9-12 VISUAL ARTS STANDARD 4: Understanding the visual arts in relation to history and cultures

GRADE 9-12 VISUAL ARTS STANDARD 5: Reflecting upon and assessing the characteristics and merits of their work and the work of others

GRADE 9-12 VISUAL ARTS STANDARD 6: Maiming connections between visual arts and other disciplines

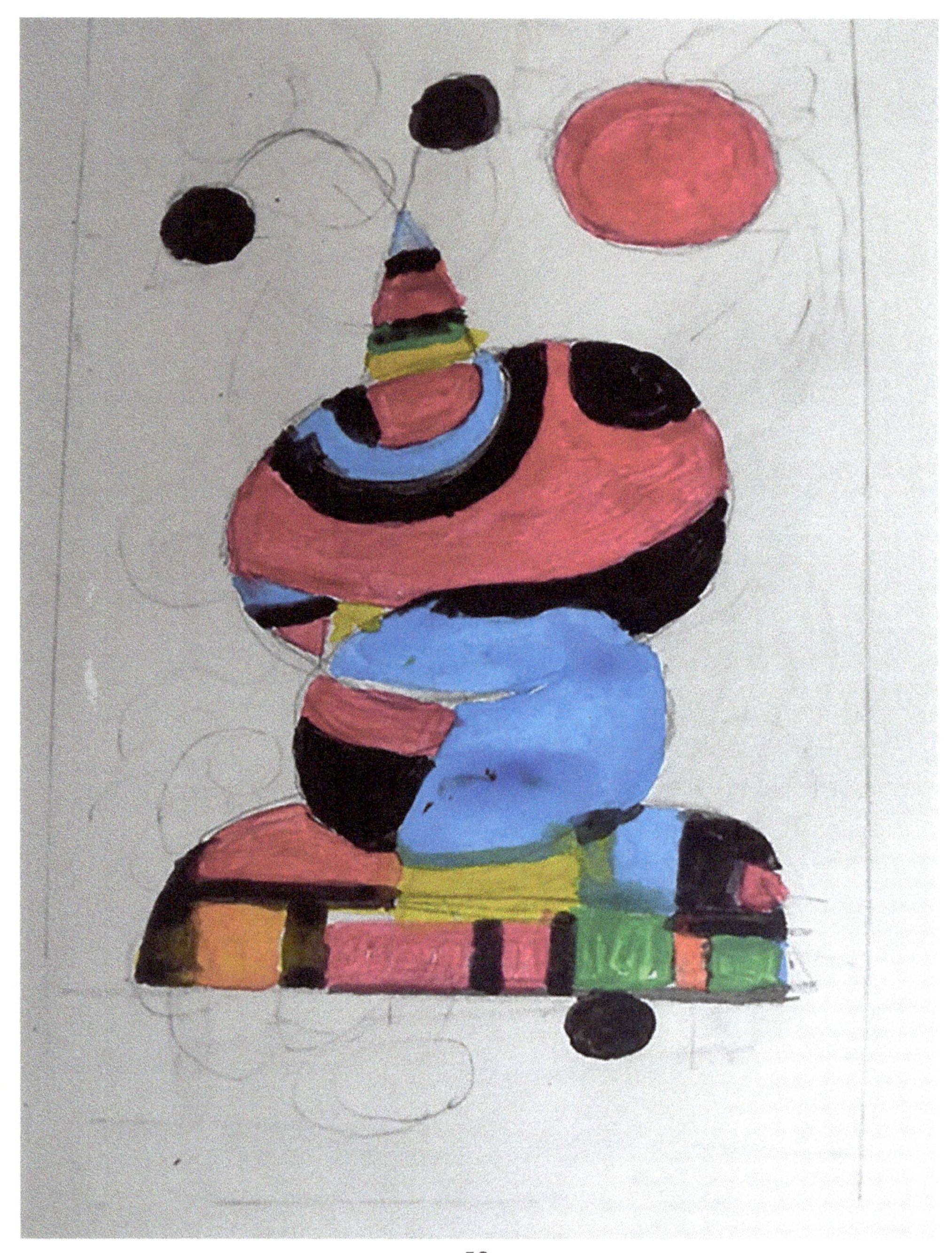

LESSON PLAN FOR DAY EIGHT

1.5 HOURS -90 MINUTES

NAME OF LESSON: Putting It All Together/Art History Portraits Time-Line

GRADE LEVEL: Junior College

SUBJECT: ESL/Art

COURSE OVERVIEW: Self-Portraits Through Ages of Art History is a course that will provide context for English language Learners to experience self-discovery through the venue of art. When art is incorporated into the E$L core curriculum it enhances students' engagement and comprehension, increases whole-brain activity, and challenges overall growth in the learning process.

COURSE OBJECTIVES: Upon completion of this course the student will be able to identify and recognize six periods of art history, learn new vocabulary, and be able to express their feelings through the written word and oral discussions. Students will expedence self-discovery, and create self-portraits through the venue of art.

In Lesson Plan #8 Students will take a final assessment test in order to check their overall progress and comprehension. Students will work in cooperative groups and create a visual timeline which will cover each art history period and artist studied following their final assessment exam. Students' self-portraits (which have been depicted in various media) will be displayed directly alongside their written expressive work and put in chronological order. Students should have the option to display their art and written work in a display case at the college and as an extension of differentiated instruction at the downtown public library. Students should feel that they have created a unique artwork of which they can be proud of.

Overview of Lesson	10 Minutes	Instructional Input	Teacher demonstrates how to construct visual timeline of students' self- portraits and written work in chronological order.
Examples and Graphics of Art History Timeline Handouts	20 Minutes	Guided Practice	Students and teachers will work together and start drawing visual timeline and in turn mark the art and written works in chronological order.
Materials: The Illustrated Timeline of Art History: A Crash Course in Words & Pictures Turtleback by Carol Strickland PhD	20 Minutes	Vocabulary: Culture Aesthetic Social attitudes Political - laws	Teacher will give final assessment exam based upon vocabulary words, artists, and materials that students have been studying through these four weeks of six periods of art history.
Activities - Students work together cooperatively to put together a timeline	10 Minutes	Independent Practice	Students gather self-portraits & written work. Students collaborate to arrange works in chronological order in a visually pleasing manner.
Student Break	10 Minutes		Time for a little relaxation
Discussion Groups: Students work in cooperative groups to create a timeline.	20 Minutes	Closing/Student Reflection/Real Life Connections	Once students have finished drawing the visual timelines, they will decide how to place their written worlds and art. Students will transport all completed works to a display *case* within the college. In concluding this course, students will be able to share their self-discovery learning experiences through the venue of art. (For all to see)
Differentiated Instruction		Differentiated Instruction	Students can add images (from Internet) connecting to major world events - new technologies - inventions.

Course Reading: Part III pages 105-119

EDUCATIONAL STANDARDS ADDRESSED:

WIDA' *s* 2012 *Amplification of the English Language Development Standards, Kindergarten-trade 12* ("WIDA ELD Standards") is owned by the Board of Regents of the University of Wisconsin System on behalf of the WIDA Consortium. fi 2012 Board of Regents of the University of Wisconsin System, on behalf of the WIDA Consortium-www.wida.us.

WIDA ELD Standards: Standard I: Social & Instructional Language: Informed Decisions College & Career

CONNECTION: *Common Core Reading Standards for Informational Texts, Integration of Knowledge* and *Ideas* #7. Integrate and Evaluate multiple sources of information presented in different media or formats (e.g. visually, quantitatively) as well as in words in order to address a question or solve a problem.

NATIONAL STANDARDS FOR ARTS EDUCATION: The standards outline what every K-12 student should know and be able to do in the arts. The standards were developed by the Consortium of National Arts Education Association

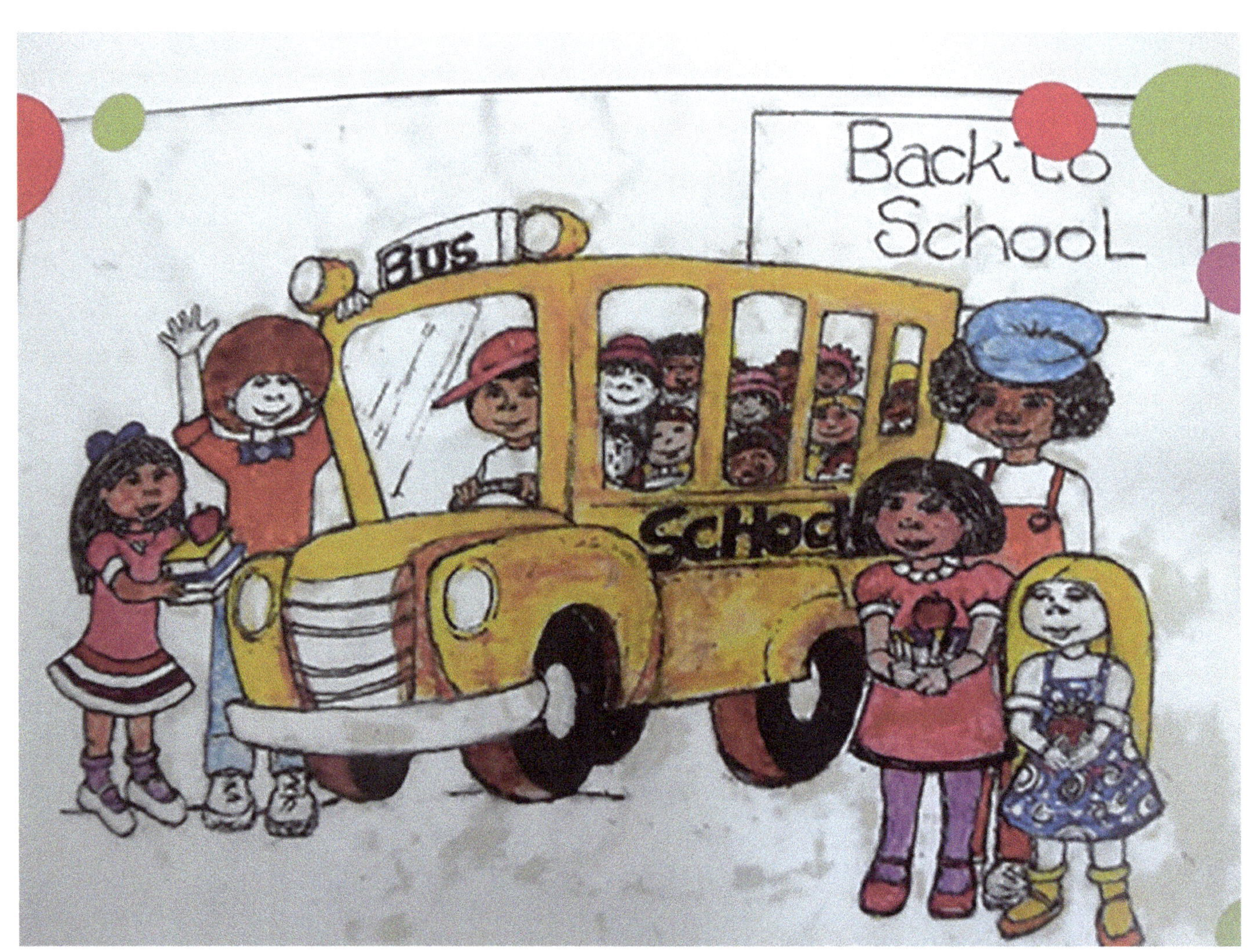

Bus
Back to
School
SchooL

GRADE 9-12 VISUAL ARTS STANDARD 1: Understanding and applying media, techniques, and processes

GRADE 9-12 VISUAL ARTS STANDARD 2: Using knowledge of structures and functions

GRADE 9-12 VISUAL ARTS STANDARD 3: Choosing and evaluating a range of subject matter, symbols, and ideas

GRADE 9-12 VISUAL ARTS STANDARD 4: Understanding the visual arts in relation to history and cultures

GRADE 9-12 VISUAL ARTS STANDARD 5: Reflecting upon and assessing the characteristics and merits of their work and the work of others

GRADE 9-12 VISUAL ARTS STANDARD 6: Making connections between visual arts and other disciplines

www.ingramcontent.com/pod-product-compliance
Lightning Source LLC
Chambersburg PA
CBHW040857070726
47599CB00035B/2027